"Thanks to Peter Lik
who introduced me to
the panoramic format
and through his own
brilliant images gave me
the inspiration and the
encouragement to go
out and do it for myself.
Over the past two years
I have enjoyed trying to
capture the many
moods of Byron and the
surrounding area that
is enjoyed by such a
diversity of people from
around the world."

Paul Hamilton

 PeterLikPublishing

PO Box 2529 Cairns Queensland 4870 Australia
Telephone: (07) 4053 9000   **Fax:** (07) 4032 1277
sales@peterlik.com.au   **www.peterlik.com.au**

 PeterLikPublishing (SEQ)

11 Florence St Newstead Queensland 4006
Telephone: (07) 3854 0944   **Fax:** (07) 3854 0922
seq@peterlik.com.au   **www.peterlik.com.au**

© **Peter Lik Publishing**   BK18

ISBN 1876 585 06-4

Front cover - Aerial of Cape Byron and Byron Bay
Back cover - View of first light from Australia's most easterly point.
Additional photography - Murray Waite, Dave Paton, Rhonda Kay

BYRON BAY

In 1770, explorer Captain Cook sighted the Cape Byron Headland and named it 'Cape Byron'. Located at Australia's most easterly point, Byron Bay evolved from a settlement whose main industries were cedar cutting, logging, dairy and pig farming and whaling in the mid-1800s to become internationally famous for its cosmopolitan style and alternative lifestyle. The century-old Cape Byron Lighthouse still guards the headland and has become an instantly recognisable symbol of this beautiful coastal town.

Located 800km north of Sydney on some of the most spectacular coastline in Australia, Byron Bay is a haven of stunning beaches with a lively town centre which literally pulses with life. There are fire dancers, sand carvers, street entertainers and live bands, casual cafes as well as fine restaurants, exclusive resorts and unique shops, galleries and colourful markets selling locally products arts and crafts.

A mecca for backpackers, Byron Bay's permanent population of around 9000 swells year-round with visitors from all over the world drawn by its beautiful beaches and idyllic lifestyle. The climate is ideal for year round outdoor activities including surfing, windsurfing, snorkeling, kayaking, fishing, canoeing, hang gliding, golf, land-based whale watching, sailing, bowling, white water rafting or just lazing on the beaches.

Ancient volcanic activity created Byron's spectacular hinterland of World Heritage-listed National Parks, subtropical rainforests and waterfalls, ideal for self driven or 4WD guided tours and bushwalking. The awesome peak of Mt Warning dominates the hinterland landscape.

A popular beach walk is from the centre of town, along Clarks Beach to The Pass, and then via walking tracks to the lighthouse.

The Cape Byron Headland Reserve, with its dramatic cliffs, views and sheltered rainforest gullies.

The first light of a new day touches the Cape Byron Lighthouse.

The Cape Byron Lighthouse is a popular spot for whale and dolphin watching.

The hilly slopes surrounding the lighthouse are home to a colony of mountain goats.

Clarks Beach is a quieter alternative to nearby Main Beach.

A bird's eye view of Byron Bay looking inland to the Hinterland.

Aerial view of Byron Bay looking south to Broken Head and Lennox Head.

The laid-back Byron Bay Beach Hotel is a popular drawcard for locals and visitors.

Playful dolphins are a common and breathtaking sight off Byron's beaches.

Previous page: Wreck Beach is home to a surf break featuring the wreck of the SS Woollongbar.

Whale watchers are rewarded with the spectacle of a double breech.

Crystal clear waters and year-round sunshine make Byron a paradise for water activities.

A surfer makes the most of the last light at The Pass, as the sun sets on Mt Warning.

The walking track to The Pass offers great views of Wategos Beach.

The Julian Rocks Aquatic Reserve is a popular diving and snorkelling spot, just off the coast from Byron Bay.

An abundance of underwater wildlife can be found at Julian Rocks.

Byron Bay Beach Hotel.

Previous page: Dive boats bound for Julian Rocks are launched in spectacular style at The Pass.

The Byron Bay Visitor Centre is housed in the old railway stationmaster's cottage.

Byron Bay has a surprisingly cosmopolitan town centre full of fine restaurants, al fresco cafes, unique shops, galleries and weekly markets.

Byron Bay's Community Centre.

A colourful Byron surf shop.

Byron's Pavilion Swimming pool kiosk, built in 1951 at Main Beach.

Aerial view of the coastal village of Brunswick Heads, a genuine fishing town. *Previous page: Brunswick Heads and south to Byron Bay from Lions Lookout, Ocean Shores.*

A peaceful spot on the banks of the Brunswick River.

The Brunswick Heads Hotel is the perfect spot for a cold beer and a great meal.

Trawlers line Fisherman's co-op at Brunswick Heads.

The Brunswick River offers a safe aquatic playground.

The small Hinterland village of Mullumbimby sits at the base of Mt Chincogan, north-west of Byron.

Surfers head for the crystal clear waters of Broken Head.

A lone pelican waits for the early morning catch at Broken Head Beach.

Lake Ainsworth, a freshwater tea tree lake, just south of Byron Bay, is a popular sailing spot.

View of Byron from the hills due west.

A hang glider launches from the coastal cliffs of Lennox Head.

HINTERLAND

Byron Bay lies within the Caldera Plate, an old shield volcano active 23 million years ago. This ancient volcanic activity has created a spectacular Hinterland of rugged mountain ranges, World Heritage-listed National Parks, subtropical rainforests, breathtaking waterfalls and panoramic views. The awesome peak of Mt Warning, a remnant of an ancient volcano, dominates the landscape and provides the ultimate challenge for bushwalkers who want to be the first in Australia to see the sun rise. Also World Heritage-listed are the Nightcap and Border Ranges National Parks which lie on the same eroded volcano rim which circles the remnant central core that is Mt Warning. A network of walking tracks guides bushwalkers and various lookouts offer stunning views over the ranges and valleys to the dazzling blue of the Pacific Ocean.

The historic village of Bangalow lies surrounded by fertile farmland.

Historic buildings, cafes, antique shops and galleries are all part of the charm of Bangalow's main street.

Minyon Falls plunge 100 metres into a deep palm shaded gorge.

A lush subtropical gully of Mt Warning National Park.

The country charm of Rosebank's General Store and Post Office is typical of the Hinterland.

The World Heritage Nightcap National Park offers subtropical and warm temperate rainforest.

The platypus is a shy mammal found in freshwater creeks and lakes.

The colourful main street of Nimbin, home of the famous Aquarius Festival and a thriving alternative community.

A psychedelic painted Kombi and murals form the colourful facade of the Nimbin Museum.

The colourful Byron and Beyond community markets are held every weekend throughout the region.

The Tweed River snakes its way through fields of sugar cane toward Murwillumbah and Mt Warning, which was named by Captain Cook in 1770.

Previous page: The peaceful early morning reflection on Clarrie Hall Dam.

Peter Lik Gallery

Multi award-winning photographer Peter Lik proudly presents his signature Galleries. The Galleries, with their handcrafted timber floors and unique custom decor radiate a beautiful ambience.

The stunning 'Gallery Collection' is selected from Peter's library of over 250,000 images and hand printed as limited edition Ilfochrome photographs.

Entering a Peter Lik Gallery is a total sensory experience. His connection with the heart and soul of the landscape is evident and he captures the true feeling of the land like no other.

CAIRNS	SYDNEY	PORT DOUGLAS	SAN FRANCISCO
4 Shields Street	QVB, 455 George St	19 Macrossan Street	Pier 39, Embarcadero
Tel **(07) 4031 8177**	Tel **(02) 9269 0182**	Tel **(07) 4099 6050**	Tel **(415) 765 7515**

BOOKS BY PETER LIK

- Australia
- Blue Mountains
- Brisbane
- Byron Bay
- Cairns
- Daintree and Cape Tribulation
- Fraser Island
- Gold Coast
- Great Barrier Reef
- Port Douglas
- Sunshine Coast
- Sydney
- The Red Centre
- Townsville and Magnetic Island
- Wildlife
- World Heritage Rainforest

LARGE FORMAT PUBLICATIONS

- "Australia - Images of a Timeless Land"
- San Francisco

 PeterLikPublishing